Original title:
Snowman Gone Rogue

Copyright © 2024 Creative Arts Management OÜ
All rights reserved.

Author: Wyatt Kensington
ISBN HARDBACK: 978-9916-94-270-3
ISBN PAPERBACK: 978-9916-94-271-0

Frosty Clarity

In a park, he took a stroll,
With a carrot nose and a heart of coal.
He waved to kids, oh what a sight,
But stole their hats, what a frosty fright!

He danced on ice with playful glee,
While chasing squirrels up a tree.
A snowball fight, he did declare,
But got pelted back; how unfair!

Frigid Dreams of Adventure

He dreamed of beaches, sun-kissed shores,
Instead, he was stuck, with winter wars.
He planned a break, a daring flight,
Wishing for some warm daylight.

With a wink and jiggle, he took the leap,
Slipping and sliding, oh what a sweep!
But all he found were frozen pools,
And schemes that left him looking like a fool!

The Legacy of the Snow Trail

His footprints led to mischief's door,
On frozen lakes, he craved much more.
He built a fortress, grand and wide,
Yet failed to see the goofy slide!

From icy peaks to valleys low,
He ruled the lands, a frosty show.
But with a splash on glittering ice,
His reign turned into a slip-and-slide heist!

Unraveling Winter's Bind

With every twisted snowball tossed,
He giggled hard, for he was lost.
In a snowmen chase, he led the pack,
Until a dog turned his fun to slack!

He dodged and darted, got caught in a flurry,
A fluffy mess! Oh, what a worry!
Yet through the chaos, laughter rang,
For mischief's tune, he sweetly sang.

Tread Lightly on the Ice

On a frosty morning, he took a dash,
With a wink and a twirl, and a cheeky splash.
He strode on the ice, much to the fright,
Of playful kids bundled up tight.

The Icicle Revolt

Hanging high from rooftops, sharp as a knife,
Icicles plotted, plotting out life.
"No more will we dangle, so cold and so clear,"
They rallied together, filled with good cheer.

Whispering Winds of Change

A gust blew past, and he danced with glee,
With floppy hat waving, wild and free.
The trees started giggling, shaking with laughter,
As he twirled in the snow, causing disaster.

Shattered Carrot Dreams

Once a proud nose, bright orange and round,
Now he's just bits scattered on the ground.
"Oh how I dreamed of a glamorous look,"
But fate had a plan, with a careless cook.

Whispers of a Frigid Insurrection

In winter's chill, he sought to play,
A frosty figure, bright and gray.
With carrot nose, and coal for eyes,
He plotted mischief 'neath the icy skies.

He donned a hat, so grand and tall,
A jolly robe, he felt so small.
He danced around as kids would cheer,
Yet deep inside, he held a sneer.

He rolled a ball of glistening frost,
While giggling loud, he paid the cost.
The snowflakes laughed at his wild spree,
A frosty riot, wild and free!

When darkness came, he made a dash,
Abandoning all in a snowy flash.
With twinkling eyes, he left behind,
A winter tale, or so we find.

The Cry of the Snowy Wanderers

In fields of white, they didn't freeze,
A band of snow, as bright as cheese.
With limbs outstretched, they took to flight,
The frosty figures danced in delight.

One wobbled left and then right too,
While others giggled, in shimmery hues.
No children near to keep them in place,
They spun around, a wild embrace!

With scarves of red and hats so snug,
They sang a tune, just like a bug.
Through frozen trees, their laughter rang,
A band of frost, in joy they sang.

But watch them closely, if you may,
For rogue and raucous be their play.
As shadows fade, when nightfall falls,
Their antics echo through the halls.

The Quest Beyond the Snowfield

A frosty quest, they took a leap,
With crazy plans, they'd never sleep.
Through snowflakes thick, and chilly air,
The icy squad slipped everywhere.

They dreamed of land where snowmen roll,
And built new friends, as silly as a shoal.
A race to see who'd dash the best,
In slushy fun, they found their jest.

To sledding hills, they hooted loud,
Creating chaos, drawing a crowd.
With a wink and spin, they took their chance,
A bizarre winter wonderland dance!

But as the stars began to gleam,
They vanished softly, like a dream.
The tracks they left, a fuzzy blur,
Of winter's jest, and joyful stir.

Witty Winter Misadventures

In fluffy crowds, the snowmen came,
With antics wild, they played a game.
A wink from one, a snowball fly,
As laughter echoed, oh my, oh my!

A snowman flipped; oh what a sight!
While others crowded, giggling bright.
A tumble here, a plop right there,
In frosty fun, they had not care.

With marshmallow heads and buttons round,
Their witty tales were so profound.
They built a castle, watch it sway,
In melting joys, they stole the day!

But come the sun, the giggles fade,
A playful hint of mischief made.
Yet in our hearts, they'll stay and play,
In every flake, they find their way.

Cold Feet

Once a frosty figure stood,
Dancing shoes made from wood.
He slipped and slid with grace,
In search of a warm embrace.

Chased a snowflake down the street,
Wore mismatched socks on his feet.
Laughing at the winter's chill,
He shook his head and said, "What a thrill!"

Warm Intentions

A carrot nose and coal for eyes,
Joked about his warm goodbyes.
Wanted sun, oh what a dream,
To melt away, oh how he'd beam.

But instead, he danced and spun,
Played hopscotch under the sun.
His frosty friends stared in shock,
"When did he start to rock?"

Mischief in the Me snow

With a wink, he stole a hat,
That's when all the fun was at.
Had a twirl, and then a jump,
Causing snowballs with a thump.

Chasing rambunctious kids around,
Spinning, laughing—what a sound!
He waved his arms, a snowy spree,
Managing a snowy jubilee.

Frozen Independence Day

With sparkly lights and a chill in the air,
He planned a party without a care.
Fireworks made of frozen snow,
An icy flag to wave on the go.

He threw confetti from his hands,
As winter raised a glass of brands.
To freedom, fun, and chilly nights,
Where laughter soared to new heights.

The Frigid Disobedience

He dreamed to skate when it was hot,
Ignoring rules, he gave it a shot.
Rolling downhill, what a sight,
Despite the chill, he felt so light.

His frosty friends yelled, "Stay put!"
But he just giggled, feeling cute.
Frosty chaos, no time to waste,
In his wacky world, he found his taste.

Rebel Without a Cause

In the yard, a frosty fella,
Breaking rules, a jolly dweller.
Wearing shades and squeaky shoes,
Spreading laughter, sharing blues.

He dances wildly, kicks the snow,
Takes a twirl, puts on a show.
Comets zoom, he sings aloud,
This snowy prankster, praise him proud!

With a carrot nose and cheeky grin,
He starts a snowball fight, let's begin!
Frosty mischief in the light,
Who knew winter could be so bright?

He rallies friends, a wintry crew,
A marching band, all made of goo.
With puffy hats and scarves askew,
We'll rule the yard, it's what we do!

The Winter Igloo Insurrection

In the corner, an igloo gleams,
But inside lurk some funny schemes.
With snow-doughnuts piled so high,
The frosty rebels laugh and sigh.

They build a fort with sticks and glee,
Planning tricks as they sip some tea.
Making snowmen act like kings,
While snowflakes dance and do their things.

A penguin joins with playful flair,
And tosses snowballs everywhere.
They laugh so hard, they can't stand tall,
The frozen fun, it breaks the wall.

They crown their chief, a clever hare,
With carrot scepter, full of flair.
This winter coup is quite the sight,
As stars peek out to join the night!

Snowflakes in the Spotlight

A stage was set with twinkling lights,
For snowflakes eager, bold in tights.
They twirled and spun, a dazzling crew,
In a dance-off, who'd win? Who knew?

One flake slipped, landed on his bum,
The crowd erupted, laughter, hum!
They honked like geese, a silly show,
With puffs of air, they stole the glow.

From fluffy clouds, they floated down,
Dressed in gowns of white, sans frown.
Imperfections made them charm the crowd,
As cheers erupted, strong and loud.

With every twist, and every flip,
They painted winter with a quip.
These snowflakes glimmered, oh so bright,
In the spotlight, they claimed the night!

A Conspiracy of Cold

With frozen hands, they plot away,
A winter's game, let's start to play.
Snowball schemes and chilly pranks,
This frosty crew has all the flanks.

They gather near the frozen pond,
With whispers soft, a pact, so fond.
Shenanigans with icicles sharp,
Their laughter echoes, songs of a harp.

Sneaky steps on the glistening ice,
A dash behind for just a slice.
Tickling toes as they glide on by,
The snowflakes giggle, oh my, oh my!

In every flurry, chaos reigns,
As chilly capers fill the veins.
This wintry rebel force, so bold,
Brought the season tales to be told!

The Ice Age Awakens

In a world of frost and chill,
A jolly figure starts to thrill.
With a carrot nose and a cheeky grin,
He plots a melting game to win.

With nimble arms made of twigs,
He dances around, doing his jigs.
No longer bound by a child's dreams,
He schemes and scuttles, bursting seams.

He steals a scarf, a hat, a glove,
Laughs at the chaos with glee thereof.
His icy smile, a frosty twist,
Brings laughter loud and frostbit bliss.

But when the sun begins to rise,
He waves goodbye, with playful sighs.
Back to the yard, where he once lay,
Tomorrow's fun will be on display.

The Playful Powder Plunder

Once stuffed with snow and pure delight,
This frosty chap took off one night.
With a wink and a grin, he set out fast,
On a playful rampage, oh what a blast!

Sledding down hills, he takes to flight,
With snowballs flying, oh what a sight!
He snags a scarf from a passing pup,
"Who knew this adventure could be such fun up?"

He captures the winds with a giggling shout,
Around town, his laughter rings out.
Kids join him on this wild spree,
A snow-capped ruckus—it's pure jubilee!

As night falls down 'neath the glowing moon,
He skips back home, humming a tune.
With a wink to his friends and a skip in his beat,
He dreams of mischief, oh isn't life sweet?

Snow-Sculpted Freedom

With frosty hands, a rebel bold,
He breaks the mold, no longer controlled.
With every stomp, each shifty sway,
He carves out laughter in his play.

From backyard chains to streets so wide,
He rolls with joy, no place to hide.
Snowflakes twirl in his merry wake,
Creating chaos, make no mistake!

A snowball clash, a snowy fight,
Blue skies gleaming, spirits bright.
In a flurry of giggles and swirling snow,
This frosty free spirit steals the show.

But as shadows stretch and stars appear,
He catches his breath and gives a cheer.
With a heart so light and a spirit so merry,
He dreams of tomorrow, oh what a fairy!

Against the Wind and Snow

With the wind against him, he takes a stand,
A mischievous heart in a frosty land.
He waddles and wobbles, a sight to behold,
In the midst of winter's icy hold.

Through swirling snowflakes, he bounds with glee,
Challenging fate like a brave little spree.
Dodging the chill with a cheeky shout,
His antics cause laughter all about!

He crafts a snow fort, the size of a castle,
Inviting all friends for a snowy tussle.
Hot cocoa dreams swirl in the air,
As the evening wraps up in a frosty flair.

With a chuckle and twinkle, he calls it a night,
His playful reign fading from sight.
But come tomorrow with the dawn's soft glow,
He'll be back to play, in the wind and the snow!

Snowball's Revolt

In the yard, with carrots bright,
The little balls conspired at night.
With tiny arms, they danced around,
Plotting mischief, without a sound.

They gathered snow, their fortress grew,
No more standing, they'd break the blue.
Laughing loudly, they rolled and spun,
The snowball fight had just begun!

The Tundra's Untamed Heart

Amidst the chill, they found their sway,
Dancing wildly, in frosty play.
The flakes were flying, laughter soared,
A winter party, hearts restored.

No time for frowns, let's make some cheer,
With snowmen breaking out of fear.
They twirled and spun, like stars on ice,
A blizzard of joy, oh, how nice!

I'd Rather Melt Than Conform

With a top hat askew, he took a stance,
Refusing to follow the frozen dance.
Said he'd rather drip than blend in,
A rebel at heart, let the antics begin!

He turned to the moon, gave a cheeky grin,
Said, 'Who needs structure? Let's spin!'
With a wiggle and jiggle, he started to sway,
Soon all the snowflakes joined in the fray!

Frosted Courage on Display

In the park, they took a brave leap,
A crew of snowfolk, no time for sleep.
With a wink and a nudge, they rolled down the hill,
Laughing so hard, they felt the thrill.

They wore wild hats, mismatched and bright,
Not caring for rules in the soft moonlight.
Through snowdrifts high, they danced with glee,
Rebels of winter, as free as can be!

March of the Snowy Outsiders

In the yard where the snow piled high,
Marshmallow hats gave a cheeky sigh.
They rolled and tumbled with glee in the night,
Waving their sticks in a silly fight.

With carrot noses held up so proud,
They dared to dance in a jolly crowd.
No children to watch, no rules to abide,
These frosty rebels were ready to ride.

They formed a line, oh what a parade,
Chasing the cat through the snow they swayed.
With giggles that echoed through dim winter skies,
The chilly mischief made everyone rise.

Yet as dawn broke, they froze in their tracks,
Caught in a pose, with no way to relax.
Dissolving dreams, in the warmth they'd grieve,
But oh what a night, such fun they believed!

Dance of the Defiant Snowflakes

Tiny flakes falling, in a sly little dance,
Swaying around with a mischievous glance.
They tickled the noses of children nearby,
As laughter erupted and spirits flew high.

With twirls and flips, they sparkled and spun,
Challenging winter to join in the fun.
Ignoring the chill, they banished the gloom,
In a whirl of white that brightened the room.

Each flake a rebel, a wild, happy crew,
They joined together, all bright and anew.
They teased at the ground, with no care at all,
Creating a blanket, a frosty white wall.

As the sun peeked out, they shouted, "Not yet!"
"Winter's our stage, and we're not done yet!"
In giggles and whirlwinds, they danced through the light,
Creating a scene that was pure winter delight!

The Spirit of Winter Rebellion

In a world full of frost, a plot thickened fast,
As winter's chill came down like a blast.
The critters all murmured, "It's time to unite,
Let's throw winter's rules out with all of our might!"

The rabbits donned scarves, the birds wore a grin,
And snow rolled its eyes, ready to spin.
Piling up marshmallows, they threw a grand bash,
Under the moody sky, with one glorious splash.

Formalities tossed, they began to defy,
With snowflakes in glittery hats floating by.
All around the warmth, the silliness grew,
As laughter erupted where nobody knew.

A snow fort was built in a glorious spree,
While everyone cheered and shouted with glee.
"Let winter take notes, we'll teach them to play,
With laughter, not snowballs, we'll brighten the day!

Frost-Laden Adventures

In the depths of the night, the frost took to flight,
With boots made of ice that sparkled so bright.
They trekked through the forest, a whimsical band,
Led by a squirrel with a snowball in hand.

Through the thickets and shadows, they giggled with mirth,
With snow flurries dancing above frozen earth.
They slid down the hills, with delightful flair,
Creating a ruckus with no one to care.

And as winter would watch with a glimmering eye,
The frost-laden crew gave a jubilant cry.
"Let's show them the fun, let's cause a delight,
When snow tells a tale, it's always just bright!"

But dawn started peeking, the adventures would fade,
As frost took its leave while they happily played.
With promises of mischief for seasons to come,
They settled in stillness, their laughter, a hum.

Snowy Solstice Rebellion

In a field of winter white,
Frosty friends take flight,
With scarves and hats so grand,
They plot a snowy stand.

Balloons in the air, they rise,
Stealing snacks, oh what a surprise!
Hot cocoa stolen from the fire,
A chilly band of pure desire.

No more holding just their ground,
With giggles and laughs, they surround,
They march with carrot noses high,
And snowflakes dance from low to sky.

In the quiet night, they scheme,
Making mischief, living the dream,
Weaving tales of frosty cheer,
Defiant in their frosty sphere.

Frosted Fury's March

With brooms and sticks, they take a stance,
Frosted hearts begin to dance,
Creating tricks, oh what a sight,
They prance beneath the pale moonlight.

Mischief reigns in snowy lanes,
Frosty foes release their chains,
With snowballs aimed, they throw with glee,
Such winter antics, wild and free!

They shuffle past the frozen trees,
Giggling loud on the brisk breeze,
A carrot nose with a grin so wide,
As winter mischief becomes their guide.

In a flurry, they launch a raid,
Seeking treats, they're unafraid,
Who would have guessed this frozen band,
Would lead a march on sugarland?

A Winter's Defiance

Gather round for this frosty tale,
Of playful pranks that never fail,
With frosty hands and frosty feet,
They vowed no more to be discreet.

Whisked away on wind's delight,
They bumbled through the starry night,
Snowballs rolling with a clash,
In a comic twist, they made a splash.

Ideas brewed like cocoa warm,
Plans devised amidst the storm,
With giggles and the brightest cheer,
Defiance strong, they had no fear.

So if you see them in your yard,
Capering about, it's quite the card,
Just know they're rebels, bold and free,
Creating chaos, endlessly!

The Melting Whisper of Change

Once they stood so proud and tall,
Now they giggle through the fall,
With sunshine beaming, they can't resist,
The lure of warmth, they can't just twist.

Carrot noses wiggling bright,
They plot to dance with sheer delight,
To slide on ice and break the mold,
As temperatures rise, their stories unfold.

Sipping tea with mugs so fine,
Planning adventures in every line,
They shrug off frost with a playful cheer,
In every melt, there's naught to fear.

So as the winter days retreat,
Watch for laughter, funny and sweet,
The snowflakes twirl, with joy they sing,
For change is here, come what it may bring.

Perilous Powder Play

In the yard, a frosty plot,
A jolly figure, oh how it fought!
With a carrot nose, it took a stance,
But the neighbors giggled at its dance.

Snowflakes flew, those fluffy bites,
As it rolled and tumbled in pure delight.
Chasing kids with a witty grin,
A fluffy villain, this won't end well for him!

A hat askew and sticks all bent,
It marched around, its own content.
With a twirl and a spin, it did declare,
"I'm the king of snow; beware, beware!"

Now the kids all cheer and scream,
As the rebel snowball starts to scheme.
A slippery slope, the laughter spread,
Chasing the rogue till they fell instead!

Frosted Adventures Afoot

Under the moon, the snowball glows,
With mischief brewing, everyone knows.
It took a leap, so wild and free,
In search of fun, it called to me!

Carrot rebels lined up in rows,
As our frosty friend struck a pose.
With arms outstretched, it waved around,
And whirled to the sound of joy abound.

Through the yard, it sped so fast,
Leaving tracks, a comical blast.
Rolling over, causing quite a scene,
With snowballs flying like a dream!

It took a bow and winked just right,
As snowflakes danced in moon's soft light.
The neighborhood burst into laughter loud,
At the antics of the frosty crowd!

Dancing Through the Drifts

In the wintry night, the fun began,
A rebel shape with a frosty plan.
It shook its body, what a sight,
Sliding on ice, pure delight!

With twirls and spins, it ruled the scene,
This frosted dancer, so evergreen.
Hands made of sticks, a hat askew,
Brought giggles forth, oh yes, it flew!

It bopped and hopped through the wintery cold,
Each frosty move, a story told.
Snowflakes swirled in laughter's cheer,
As the rogue rebel brought good cheer!

From driveway to yard, it spread its glee,
A frolicsome friend, so wild and free.
As dawn sneaked in, the dance was done,
Leaving behind sheer trails of fun!

The Flake That Stood Tall

A fluffy figure with such bold flair,
Stood under sunlight, caught unaware.
With a crooked grin and eyes so wide,
It sparked adventures, nowhere to hide!

Gathering kids for a raucous game,
It frolicked forth, never looking the same.
In leaps and bounds, it strutted around,
Creating laughter, what a joyful sound!

But soon its plan went awry in delight,
As slippery slopes led to a snowy fright.
With tumbling joy, it lost its cool,
Rolling around like a jolly fool!

At day's end, the laughter rang,
With warm hearts even as the cold stang.
For in the yard, that bold frosty ball,
Was the funniest friend—the flake so tall!

The Misadventures of a Frosty Renegade

One frosty night, he took a stroll,
Waving his stick, feeling quite whole.
He stuck out his arms, ready to dance,
Wobbling around like he's got a chance.

Neighbors gasped, kids ran inside,
As he rolled away, they felt the tide.
With a carrot nose and his button eyes,
He said, "I'm free! No need for goodbyes!"

Down the street, he found a snowball,
Made a big hit, had the best brawl.
Sunshine peered through, but he didn't care,
He was the captain of his snowy lair.

In the park, he climbed on a sled,
Racing past kids, filling them with dread.
"Catch me if you can," he yelled with glee,
This frosty renegade, wild and free.

Glacial Uprising

In the heart of winter, a plan was laid,
All the snowflakes joined, none afraid.
"No man can hold us down!" they cheered,
With a furry resolve, their mission steered.

One depicted a snowman, round and stout,
"Let's break our chains, kick winter out!"
They danced upon rooftops, covered in fluff,
While parents watched, saying, "This is tough!"

The ice and snow band erupted in song,
Tickling toes where they did not belong.
A blizzard swirled as they hit the streets,
Rusty skateboards and fluffy snow feats.

Laughter erupted as they spun and whirled,
In a frosty revolution, they twirled and twirled.
No care for the cold, only joy and fun,
In this wild winter, the snowflakes won!

Melting Chains of Winter

With the sun on the rise, he felt a shift,
Waving goodbye to his icy gift.
"I refuse to melt, oh no, not me!"
He built a fortress, as proud as can be!

He gathered his mates, each a cold sprite,
Holding a meeting deep in the night.
"Together we'll stand, we'll fight for our lives,
We'll steal summer's thunder, and dance with our jives!"

They built a tower, made of fresh snow,
Built it up high—it began to glow.
They painted it bright, made it flashy and bold,
Screaming, "Take that! We won't be controlled!"

As the sun beamed down, they wiggled with flair,
But slippery antics made them declare,
"Maybe melting ain't so bad after all,
As we slide down the hill, let the good times roll!"

The Frosted Runaway

One day he decided to ditch his post,
"Too much sun! I'm not a frosty ghost!"
He packed his stuff, a scarf and a hat,
With a little cart, he rode off, just like that.

Through the neighborhood, he rolled with cheer,
Leaving trails of giggles, spreading good gear.
Kids chased him down the frosty lane,
Hoping to catch him, but he felt no pain.

He found a park, threw caution aside,
Flipping and flopping, oh what a ride!
On a slippery slope, he did a twist,
Came crashing down—oops! No way to resist.

With laughter echoing across the snow,
He kicked up puffs, what a bright show!
The runaway frost, with a heart so bold,
Stirred up mischief, and stories untold.

Flakes of Anarchy

In a field of white, he stood so tall,
With a scarf of red, he wanted it all.
Carrots misplaced, a cheeky grin wide,
Causing pure chaos, he took off with pride.

Snowballs were flying, laughter erupted,
Kids chased him down, all plans disrupted.
He danced through the drifts, with a silly jig,
Leaving behind him a snow-covered gig.

With each little tumble, he'd squeak and he'd roll,
A rebel with buttons, he's playful and whole.
Through snowflakes and giggles, he's spreading delight,
Under the moon, he plans his next flight.

Mischievous antics, he caught every eye,
Making the cold days feel warm, oh my!
The winter was crazy, but joy was in store,
A rogue made of frost, we all want him more!

The Snowborn Rebellion

Once in a yard, a hero was made,
With a broom for a sword and a hat that swayed.
He led a revolt, the children did cheer,
A snowy uprising with laughter so clear.

Buttons for armor, they took to the street,
Hurling soft snowballs at anyone they meet.
Neighbors looked puzzled, what's happening here?
As giggles and snowflakes filled the bright air.

Their laughter was loud, as they rolled in the snow,
Creating chaos, stealing the show.
A legendary tale of frosty delight,
As they marched on, through the cold, starry night.

The bravest of frosty, a true snow hero,
Challenging winter, he earned his bravado.
A champion of joy, for fun he will fight,
In a world made of snow, he'll shine ever bright.

Umbrella of Frost

A snowball of mischief with a sly little wink,
He caught some bright flakes as he danced in a blink.
With an umbrella in hand, he twirled all around,
Creating a ruckus with joyfully bound.

Through parks covered icy, he juggled with glee,
A lad full of laughter as wild as could be.
With each little slip, he broke into cheer,
A frosty sensation, spreading the fun near.

Snowflakes their best friends, they swirled in delight,
As they joined in the madness that lit up the night.
He tossed up a flurry, and shouted with zest,
For winter had never been funner, you guessed!

With a twinkle of mischief, he stole the scene,
A whimsical frosty, playful and keen.
Under the moonlight, he danced with a spin,
An umbrella of frost, let the fun begin!

The Great Winter Takeoff

With a flurry of giggles, up he would soar,
A dashing little figure, who dreamed of that door.
He built a fine sleigh made of ice and delight,
Declaring adventure on a cold, starry night.

With a hoot and a laugh, he called all his friends,
"For a journey of joy, the laughter never ends!"
So they hopped in together, a crowd full of cheer,
Whisking through snowflakes, with not a hint of fear.

Up into the skies, they twinkled and spun,
Creating a whirlwind of frosty, pure fun.
Through clouds made of sugar, they danced in the air,
A winter escapade, full of joy and flair.

As they soared through the twilight, hearts warm and light,
With a splash of white giggles, oh what a sight!
The great winter flight was a legend to share,
Of a frosty rebellion, beyond any compare!

The Frostbitten Freedom Trail

In the yard, he had a hat,
But decided it was time for that.
With a twirl and a jolly leap,
He shimmied away, not making a peep.

Down the street, past the pines,
He dodged the kids, skated on lines.
Shaking off the snowflakes' grip,
His carrot nose took a daring trip.

He found a mug, filled with cheer,
Sipped hot cocoa with frosty sneer.
Joking with the birds on the way,
Laughing as they started to sway.

But dusk arrived, his fun was brief,
Slipping back with mischief and grief.
A lesson learned from his spree,
"Next time, I'll bring a buddy with me!"

Mischief in the Snow

Under moonlight, he came to plot,
A snowball fight, oh what a thought!
With a flick and a roll, away he danced,
The neighborhood kids stood, entranced.

He grabbed a branch, it turned to sword,
A snowy knight, he swung and scored.
They chased him down, a giggling chase,
He dodged and weaved, like in a race.

They threw their snowballs with all their might,
But he was clever, quick as a kite.
"What's your aim?" he called with glee,
"Try again, you'll have to catch me!"

At last, the sun began to rise,
With frosted laughter, they said their goodbyes.
A rogue by dawn, but friends by day,
He winked and vanished, in a snowy way.

Lost in the Winter's Whisper

One frosty eve, he shed his guise,
Trading cold for festive highs.
With a scarf swaying wild and free,
He danced through snow like a jubilee.

Whispers hummed, the night so bright,
Snowflakes spun in pure delight.
He found a sled, oh what a thrill,
Riding down the hill, he took that spill!

The children laughed, they couldn't resist,
As he tumbled and twisted, a snowy mist.
"Let's build a fort!" they shouted with glee,
He joined in, feeling so carefree.

But cheeky as he was, he had a plan,
To prank the kids, if he only can.
He fluffed up the snow, then quietly hid,
Popped out to scare—oh, what a bid!

The Chill of Rebellion

In his frosty world, he made a stand,
With a mischievous grin and a grand old band.
Snowflakes cheered as he took the leap,
"Let's break the rules, let's make it deep!"

He led a crew of snow-sculpted kin,
Planning mischief with a cheeky grin.
"Hooray for shenanigans!" he declared,
"Our frosty rebellion cannot be scared!"

They rolled and tossed in a winter's jest,
Fluffy snow angels, they did their best.
Creating chaos, they danced anew,
With giggles and laughter, the night only grew.

But just as dawn began to rise,
The warmth of day brought sleepy sighs.
With one last laugh, they bid adieu,
Until next winter, it's time to renew!

The Frostbitten Uprising

The carrots marched with icy glee,
Top hats waving, wild and free.
Coal eyes glinted with mischief bold,
As winter's magic began to unfold.

Jolly ol' snowflakes danced in fright,
While frosty rebels planned their night.
They plotted against the shovels and brooms,
In search of warmth, they'd meet their dooms.

With a twirl and a flip, they did ignite,
A snowball fight under the pale moonlight.
Innocent giggles filled the chill,
As they dodged the frost with a cheeky thrill.

So here's to the frosted brigade with sass,
Making mischief with every pass.
When winter's chill brings forth delight,
They frolic on, a snowman's plight!

White Mischief Unleashed

In the yard, they formulated plans,
To escape their cold and frosty tans.
One hat bobbed, and one scarf flew,
'Let's make a break! We have things to do!'

Down the street, a snowball rolled,
As they giggled and squeaked, feeling bold.
Snowflakes sparking like little stars,
Turning quiet nights into wild bazaars.

With flurry of laughter, they played hide and seek,
Beneath the moonlight, they felt so sleek.
An icy twirl, a chilly jig,
They formed a line, all smooth and big.

The neighbors peeped from frosted doors,
Shocked by the sights of frosty roars.
Yet the rebels frolicked without a care,
In a winter wonderland, not meant to share!

Glacial Dreams Unbound

Beneath the stars, rebellion brewed,
Frosty figures, in laughter stewed.
No longer bound by their frozen fate,
They set their sights on a snowy plate.

In the moon's glow, they seized the night,
With frozen dreams that took to flight.
Pine trees giggled, the lanterns glowed,
As winter's warriors improvised code.

On skates made of ice and pure delight,
They zipped and zoomed in the frosty bite.
Tickling snowflakes with frosty cheers,
Flipping past winter and all its fears.

A party erupted, with no regrets,
As snowmen rebels cast off their nets.
One last laugh, one final cheer,
In glacial dreams, they disappeared!

The Icecapade of Freedom

With a wink and a nod, they hatched their scheme,
To frolic freely, a snowy dream.
They fashioned a sled from a garden chair,
And sped through drifts without a care.

The neighborhood laughed, in shock and glee,
As snowy misfits rolled past the tree.
With gleeful shouts and playful spins,
They juggled the snow and welcomed wins.

Dancing and prancing, hearts all aglow,
Making snow angels in a moonlit show.
No longer frozen in place by the sun,
These cheeky cold spirits knew how to run.

So let us remember those winter nights,
When snow and mischief led to delights.
With laughter echoing through frosty space,
The icecapade brought a smile to the face!

The Shiver of Rebellion

With a carrot nose all askew,
He plotted mischief, it's true.
No more standing, frozen and stiff,
Time to dance, the frosty rift!

He wobbled and slid on frozen ground,
In his frosty heart, joy was found.
Juggling snowballs, he gave a cheer,
Shouted, "Winter, let's make this clear!"

Children laughed as he made a face,
His snow-painted antics set the pace.
Snowflakes giggled in swirling delight,
As he twirled into the chilly night!

Now every night when blankets spread,
He sneaks out, ready to spread dread.
With snowball fights and laughter loud,
A rebel formed, he feels so proud!

Tumble of Tundra's Tale

In a field of white where snowflakes plume,
He rumbled and rolled, a snowy boom.
A tumble here, a flip and a laugh,
Creating chaos, a frosty gaffe!

He leaped over fences, all filled with cheer,
Annoying the elves, they'd scurry in fear.
With a mischievous wink and a powdery grin,
The great snowy dance adventure begins!

Snowballs unleashed, they flew through the air,
Each icy missile, he hadn't a care.
Dancing with penguins, he hummed a tune,
While plotting his antics beneath the moon.

In the whispers of night, his giggles would ring,
As frost on the window danced with a fling.
So if you see snow, don't just look close,
There might be a frosty friend, a playful ghost!

Frosty Nights and Starlit Dreams

Frosty nights held secrets profound,
In the moonlight, trouble was found.
With eyes like coal, he strolled on by,
Whispering tales to the starlit sky!

He dashed through the pines, a blur of white,
Creating a wonder in the moonlight.
With every step, the magic grew,
With sparkles of snow, all fresh and new.

Next, he challenged the northern breeze,
Spinning and twirling with snow-covered trees.
"What's life without fun?" he laughed with glee,
As the night tickled his frosty glee.

Dancing on rooftops, a waltz in the night,
He sprinkled stardust, a glorious sight.
So watch for the giggles beneath the moon,
For frosty dreams are here all too soon!

The Wondrous Winter Whirl

A blustery wind sang a jolly tune,
As he whirled in the air, a playful boon.
With flurry and flair, he danced on the hill,
Creating a scene that gave everyone a thrill!

Snowflakes laughed, blowing round and about,
As he twirled on the ground, there was never a doubt.
With each giggle, he leaped and he spun,
In the winter's embrace, all frosty fun!

Carefree spirit, he chased the snow,
Throwing snowballs with a cheeky glow.
The village below watched with delight,
As he cavorted beneath the pale moonlight.

And when morning did wake, with sunshine anew,
He'd hide in the brush, waiting for a view.
For tomorrow he'll rise, with a wink and a swirl,
Oh, the joys of a wanderer in winter's whirl!

The Last Stand of the Icicle

An icicle perched on the roof's ledge,
Dreaming of freedom, it made a pledge.
No longer it hung, in frost's tight grip,
It swayed and it danced, like a merry ship.

With a mischievous twirl, it sprang to the ground,
But the splash of cold water soon brought it down.
A puddle of laughter, its final scene,
A surly icicle, no longer obscene.

Whitewashed Freedom

In a yard of white, where the snowflakes flurry,
A rogue with a broom caused such a big worry.
He painted the world in a coat of bright white,
While neighbors all gasped, what a wild sight!

He danced around, with a grin ear to ear,
Then slid on the ice with a wobble of cheer.
What craziness brewed, in the chill of the night,
A rebel in snow, what delight and fright!

Chilly Heart

A snowman so cool, with a frosty heart,
Decided one day he would play the part.
He took off his scarf, let his buttons fall,
Said, "Who needs a hat? I'll just take them all!"

With a wig made of leaves, and a grin so wide,
He flipped up his nose, and he slicked with pride.
On a wild escapade, he danced through the park,
As children all laughed at this chilly remark.

Fiery Whim

A snowman dreamed of a life so hot,
He built himself wings, gave 'red' a shot.
With a flamethrower grin, he took to the sky,
Chasing after the sun, oh my, oh my!

Around and around, in his fiery flight,
Soon melted away in that warm, sunny light.
What a silly spectacle, a sight to behold,
A sun-kissed adventure, brave and bold!

Frosty Rebel's Journey

With buttons of mischief and eyes of pure glee,
A frosty wanderer set off, you see.
He skated on puddles, played tag with the sun,
In a world that thought winter was all about fun.

Through forests of snow, and valleys of ice,
He twirled and he whirled, oh isn't it nice?
A jester of winter, with laughter so sweet,
In the heart of the chill, he embraced the beat.

The Snowy Secrets Beneath

In the yard, a figure stands tall,
With a carrot nose, he greets one and all.
But wait, what's that? A mischievous grin,
He's plotting some chaos, let the games begin!

A snowball fight? Oh, he won't forget,
Launches one first, what a crafty threat!
His twig arms flail, he dances about,
Who knew a snowman could cause such a rout?

Beneath the surface, secrets unfold,
His frosty heart beats, oh so bold!
Laughing with glee, he twirls in delight,
Making snow angels till late in the night.

So when you build him, beware the fun,
He may just turn into a wild little pun!
Frosty mischief, a chilly surprise,
With snowy secrets and sparkling eyes!

Frosty Pranks and Wandering Spirits

There once was a snowman, spry and sprightly,
With a scarf so bright, he danced tightly.
But when the moon rose, he'd change his tune,
Dashing through snow with a cheeky cartoon.

He'd knock over sleds and spin on his head,
While children inside stayed cozy in bed.
With a wink and a twirl, he'd dive down the hill,
His frosty antics, enough to thrill!

A snowball brigade, oh what a sight,
He'd lead the charge, full of frosty delight.
He'd hop and he'd skip, a rogue in the night,
Leaving a trail of laughter in flight.

So if you spot him, join in the fun,
Frosty pranks before the day's done.
With snowflakes swirling, and giggles anew,
Those wandering spirits come out just for you!

Winter's Unruly Feast

In a world of white, where mischief runs free,
A snowman sets up for a feast, oh me!
With snow for a table and icicles for forks,
He invites all the critters from nearby parks.

The rabbits bring carrots, the squirrels, acorns,
While birds chirp tunes as if we're adorned!
But the snowman smiles, he has more in store,
A whipped cream avalanche, oh, he'll roar!

With whipped frosty clouds and laughter so bright,
They feast in a flurry 'neath the moonlight.
Snowballs for snacks, and ice slush to sip,
This winter's affair makes all spirits flip!

Yet as dawn approaches, the party must end,
The snowman bows with a laugh and a bend.
His feast may be gone, but memories last,
Of winter's unruly, delicious feast blast!

The Blizzard's Bold Goodbye

As the blizzard blows wild with fury and glee,
A snowman stands proudly, as bold as can be.
With a wink and a nod, he plans his escape,
For it's time to disperse—what a daring reshape!

He leans to the left, then to right he will sway,
In a flurry of laughter, he'll dance his way.
His carrot nose twitches, watch out, run fast!
For this frosty rebel is having a blast!

The snowflakes whirl and the winds start to cheer,
He twirls in delight, without any fear.
With a pirouette, he bids the world adieu,
Leaving trails of joy as he skedaddles through!

So when winter departs, and the sun starts to glow,
Remember the snowman who stole the show.
With memories made, and giggles to share,
The blizzard's bold goodbye, beyond compare!

Unveiling Frosty Fortunes

In the chill of a bright white day,
Frosty had plans, oh what a display!
With a carrot for a nose, he'd strut with glee,
Crafting a snowball aimed right at me!

With a cap on his head and shades so cool,
He danced by the kids, making them drool.
Laughter erupted, their faces turned red,
As he launched that snowball—oh, aim for the head!

His eyes sparkled bright with a mischievous gleam,
Chasing the children, like some wild dream.
Frosty was bold, he had quite the flair,
Causing snow-fights with a flair so rare!

But when the sun shone, he made a quick run,
Dodging the warmth, oh, just for the fun!
With a wink and a grin, he vanished from view,
Leaving behind a world snowy and new!

When Snow Falls Astray

When snow falls softly, it brings such delight,
But not for our friend who decided to fight.
Rolling with laughter, he plotted a scheme,
To throw snow at the kids—oh, what a dream!

His top hat was crooked, in need of some care,
As he snuck by the trees, plotting to scare.
With snowballs in hand, he took his best shot,
And ducked behind bushes with a slick little plot!

The children all squealed, "What was that? Quick, look!"
As Frosty giggled behind the storybook.
His giggles erupted, like bubbles in air,
With snowflakes around him, they danced in his hair!

But as daylight faded and shadows grew long,
He shuffled away with a curious song.
The legend of Frosty, so wild and spry,
Would linger forever, like dreams in the sky!

The Ice Capers of a Free Soul

In a frosty land where the wild winds roam,
Frosty decided he'd find his own home.
With a twirl and a slide, he leapt with delight,
Challenging winter to join in his flight!

He made frosty friends from the snowflakes around,
Together they skated, their laughter unbound.
With each icy prank, they brought cheer to the day,
Sledding on rooftops, all in merry play!

With a wink and a smile, he dashed through the park,
Bringing giggles and joy long after it was dark.
With snow-covered mischief and dreams yet to share,
Frosty found freedom in the cold, crisp air!

As the moon shone bright, casting shadows so wide,
He danced with delight in his snowy snow-slide.
A spirit so lively, born to frolic and play,
In a world made of magic, he'd never decay!

The Secret Life of Snowy Mischief

By night in the garden where snowflakes cascade,
Frosty conspired, in shadows he played.
With a wink and a nod, he plotted with care,
To sprinkle some fun in the still, frosty air!

He gathered the snow, pack it nice and tight,
Building snow forts for a marvelous fight.
With bolts of white fury, they threw through the night,
Making sure every throw was just perfectly slight!

With every soft chuckle, the laughter rang clear,
As the stars overhead sparkled full of cheer.
Frosty, the jester, with his mischievous streak,
Was the king of the snow, and he played hide and seek!

But come dawn's first light, with a quick little wave,
He'd melt into puddles, oh, how he was brave!
Leaving vague whispers of fun still in tow,
A legend of laughter, left in the snow!

The Glacial Instincts of Liberation

In a yard, he breaks the mold,
Waving arms, a sight to behold.
With a carrot nose and coal for eyes,
He plans a dance under winter skies.

Mittens flying, he takes a chance,
Twists and turns in a frozen prance.
The kids all shout, 'What a delight!'
While he twirls away into the night.

His top hat tipped, a sneaky grin,
A rebel heart, let the frosty fun begin.
Snowflakes twirl, and laughter glows,
As he plays tricks on timid crows.

From snowball fights to leaps like a deer,
He's got a taste for winter cheer.
With whimsy bright on a chilly spree,
A frosty fiend, so wild and free.

Frost and Fury Anew

One frosty morn, with mischief in tow,
He stretched his limbs, a no-good show.
The girls and boys all made their plea,
'Oh no, what wildness can this be?'

He crafted bows, and arrows of ice,
Shooting snowflakes, oh so precise.
The laughter echoed from nearby streets,
As he dodged snowballs with nimble feats.

Whirling around like a whirlwind prude,
His frozen antics, quite the mood.
With pirouettes, he caused such glee,
A frosty rebel, as wild as can be.

He climbed the hill with a boastful stride,
Sliding down with laughter and pride.
The frosty air choked with giggles loud,
As he bowed to the cheering crowd.

The Snowdrift's Secret Agenda

In a drifty land of white and blue,
He hatched a plot for mischief anew.
Sticking his arms out wide and proud,
He giggled softly, absurdly loud.

With a touch of snow, he slipped and slid,
Plotting antics that no kid hid.
Sleds and laughter followed his path,
As he embraced the chaos, a frozen wrath.

He rolled right past a snowman parade,
Dancing merrily, his frosty escapade.
With a wink and a dash, he broke through the ranks,
While the crowd erupted in playful pranks.

Frosted feet and frozen cheer,
His cheeky grin, so sincere.
Through patches of white with fluffy flair,
He declared winter his wild affair.

Frozen Feats of Freedom

A puff of wind gave him a shove,
He took off like a snowball dove.
Breaking free from routines unkind,
To explore the world, snowdrift unwind.

He donned a scarf across his face,
And skated mad in a zigzag race.
Around each corner and beneath each tree,
Painting the town with whimsy glee.

Snowflakes twinkled as he spun,
A frosty jester, oh what fun!
With every stumble, the giggles grew,
For the ridiculous antics that he drew.

At last, he paused, with joy in tow,
Under a lamp's warm, shimmering glow.
In winter's heart, he claimed his throne,
A roguish spirit, forever known.

Winter's Wild Antics

A jolly figure in the snow,
With a carrot nose, he'll steal the show.
But wait, what's this? He starts to dance,
With a spinning jig, he's lost his chance!

He steals a hat, a scarf, a glove,
The kids all cheer, they really love.
He tumbles down, trips on his toes,
Laughing louder as the mischief grows!

With a hoot and a holler, he runs so free,
Chasing the children, now that's the key!
Snowballs fly, a playful spree,
Winter's wild antics in jubilee!

A frosty pirate on a sled so fly,
He sails the slopes, oh my, oh my!
With each brave leap, he shouts with glee,
This snowy rebel just won't agree!

The Frozen Protest

In a snowy field, they stand in line,
A chilly bunch, they want to shine.
With a frown and a wobble, they raise their stakes,
Demanding warmer days, oh make no mistakes!

One snowball cast hits a dog in the rear,
A frozen protest turns into cheer!
'No more cold!' they chant with pride,
As they roll around in a snowy slide.

Pinecone placards, they sway in the breeze,
With a wink and a giggle, they bring us to ease.
The ice brigade won't march away,
Until they have fun on a sunny day!

As the sun peeks out, they start to melt,
But laughing together, oh the joy they felt!
In a frosty stand-off, what a sight to see,
These frozen rebels just want to be free!

Icicle Dreams and Rebellion

A frosty rebel with a gleam in his eye,
Dreams of sunshine, oh my, oh my!
He dons a top hat, and a grin so wide,
As he plots a path to slip and slide.

In the moonlight glow, he gathers his crew,
With icicle swords, and a spirit so true.
Gliding swiftly on a makeshift sleigh,
They crash the hut on their wild getaway!

With laughter echoing through the cold night,
A band of snow shapes, what a sight!
The stars above shine down on their play,
Icicle dreams in a whimsical way!

But morning arrives, they fade in the light,
Yet memories linger, oh what a night!
These frosty comrades will always inspire,
A spirit of fun that will never tire!

Unruly White

Oh, the white stuff has a mind of its own,
With tumbling mischief, like seeds it's sown.
Snowflakes whisper, 'Let's cause some fun,'
As they plot together under the sun.

A mountain of fluff, they stack up high,
With snowball fights that explode and fly.
Each fluffy ball, a missile of cheer,
Unruly white, what do we hold dear?

Around the trees, they dart and dash,
Creating giggles as they crash and smash.
With snow-dusted faces, they grin with glee,
A wild white scuffle, come play with me!

As chill winds blow through the frosty air,
They huddle tight, in their playful lair.
With whimsy and laughter, take your flight,
This unruly season keeps spirits bright!

Unraveled Night

Under the moon, a misfit parade,
Snowflakes gather, in costumes displayed.
With flamboyant hats and a wild twirl,
They dance in the night, spinning and whirl!

The lanterns glow with a giggly hum,
As they leap and prance, an ensemble of fun.
Frosty feet tap on the frozen ground,
A magical moment, where joy is found.

They play in the shadows, a mischievous band,
Creating a ruckus, oh isn't it grand?
The stars overhead twinkle with delight,
At this rambunctious party, what a sight!

But come the dawn, they'll begin to fade,
Turning to tales as the sunlight invade.
Yet in our memories, they twinkle so bright,
The magic remains of that unraveled night!

Chilled Defiance

In the yard with a bucket and shovel,
He built himself into a right old trouble.
With a toppled hat, and a cheeky grin,
He plotted escape as the sun warmed in.

With a puff of snow and a squeaky laugh,
He slipped from his post on a frosty path.
Skipping the carrot, he took to the street,
On a quest for cookies, oh what a treat!

Neighbors giggled at his chilly caper,
As he danced past fences, a frosty paper.
With winter's snack clinging to his coat,
He vowed never again to be a cold-note!

Yet, as evening fell and stars gleamed bright,
He showed up at home, still full of spite.
Back to the yard with a daring shout,
He plotted his next chilly route out and about!

Frosty Footprints of Freedom

His buttons gleamed in the soft winter's light,
With a wand of a twig, he planned his flight.
By the garage and swing set, oh what a sight,
His frosty footprints led off into the night!

He rolled on the ground, twirled like a champ,
Made a snow angel while avoiding a lamp.
Dancing with glee, no one could doubt,
This was one snow fellow who was breaking out!

With a splash in the puddles, he started to cheer,
For this silly snowman had no sense of fear.
As kids chased him down with playful delight,
He spun like a top, oh, what a wild flight!

But the moon started rising, it dimmed his bright game,
And the frost in his grin began fading the same.
Back he did tumble, it's warm back at home,
And tonight he'd dream of new frosty roam!

The Ice Imbroglio

A carrot for a nose, a scarf tightly knotted,
He claimed his rebellion, thoroughly plotted.
With the kids now a-gasp, laughter echoed around,
As this chilly rogue sought to claim snowy ground.

He slipped past the gate, just like a sly fox,
Jumped over a snowdrift and surprised a box.
With a hop and a skip, he thought he might find,
Some hot cocoa fountain, or treats well-designed!

But before he could gloat about his own fame,
A dog with a wagging tail came into the game.
In a whirl of white, with a bark and a dash,
The ice imbroglio turned into a splash!

Caught between laughter and sticky paid bets,
He realized with terror, he's drowned in snowsets.
As the night chilled down, he composed in his head,
A plan for tomorrow, maybe stay home instead!

Cold-Robed Dissenter

In a snowy kingdom where winter holds sway,
A dissenter arose, and he wouldn't obey.
With a barrel for a belly and swagger so bold,
He laughed in the face of the freezing cold.

He organized crowds with a twinkle in eye,
"Let's build snow forts, we'll reach for the sky!"
Frosty folk followed, with glee in their hearts,
Children took charge, it was winter's true arts!

Together they charted a plan for escape,
With snowball decisions, each one wouldn't drape.
And while parents were fretting, "Just stay put, please!"
They embraced the warm sun with frozen-style ease!

With cheeks all aglow and laughter aflame,
They frolicked together with never a shame.
And this cold-robed figure who led them with glee,
Found freedom in snow and pure jubilee!

Frosty Rebellion

In mittened hands, he plotted schemes,
A carrot nose, with lofty dreams.
His top hat perched so bold and round,
He'd dance at night, no rules he found.

The children laughed, they turned away,
As he began to dance and sway.
With snowball fights and frosty drinks,
He'd chuckle loud, and never think.

"Oh, dare I melt? Not in my plans!
I'm ruling here, with icy hands!"
He rallied snowflakes to his side,
Against the sun, he'd surely bide.

So if you see him on the run,
Just know he's having too much fun.
A rebel in a snowy land,
Defying all with a frosty band.

The Waddle of Winter's Fury

He waddles forth with squeaky glee,
A frosty bird with no decree.
In boots too big, he stomps around,
In pure delight, he's lost and found.

With flurry in his little hat,
He tips it low and laughs at that.
A snowflake blows, it spins and flies,
He dodges it with frosty cries.

At every turn, he makes a scene,
A rogue with flair, a winter queen.
With snowball dodges and clumsy spins,
He revels loud, it's where he wins.

So watch your step when he's nearby,
A flurry of fun, he'll zoom and fly.
With laughter trailing in his wake,
A snowy strut, for joy's own sake.

A Frosted Escape

Under the moon, he'll break away,
A snowball journey for today.
With every roll and every cheer,
He plans to conquer, far and near.

His friends all shout, "Get back in line!"
"A frosty world is yours, not mine!"
But he just laughs and strikes a pose,
"No shackles here, and off he goes!"

Across the hills, he starts to dart,
With wheels of snow, he plays the part.
A slippery slope, a wild slide,
Oh! Watch him glide, with joy and pride!

So if you glimpse, that frosty face,
Just know he's found his happy place.
In snowy mischief, he paints the dark,
A funny dash, a rogue's own spark.

Rebel Against the Thaw

As springtime whispers, he shakes his fist,
"No warming sun shall sully this!"
He gathers flurries, clouds, and snow,
In winter's grasp, he'll twist and grow.

With cheeky glee, he starts to plot,
A prankster's heart, he's bold and hot.
He rolls in snow, a frosty king,
Defying thaw, he'll dance and sing.

In the park, he's got great moves,
As snowball rockets, fast he grooves.
With laughter ringing, joy unfurls,
The frozen hero, all the world!

And if the sun should dare to shine,
He'll wear shades bright, and toast with wine.
For every spring, he'll rise anew,
In fluffy fun, with frosty crew.

Milton Keynes UK
Ingram Content Group UK Ltd.
UKHW022008131124
451149UK00013B/1068

9 789916 942710